The Mastery Of Subduing The Flesh

The Mastery Of Subduing The Flesh

(THE TEACHINGS OF APOSTLE PAUL)

Oguama O. Anne

XULON PRESS

Xulon Press
2301 Lucien Way #415
Maitland, FL 32751
407.339.4217
www.xulonpress.com

© 2021 by Oguama O. Anne

All rights reserved solely by the author. The author guarantees all contents are original and do not infringe upon the legal rights of any other person or work. No part of this book may be reproduced in any form without the permission of the author. The views expressed in this book are not necessarily those of the publisher.

Due to the changing nature of the Internet, if there are any web addresses, links, or URLs included in this manuscript, these may have been altered and may no longer be accessible. The views and opinions shared in this book belong solely to the author and do not necessarily reflect those of the publisher. The publisher therefore disclaims responsibility for the views or opinions expressed within the work.

Unless otherwise indicated, Scripture quotations taken from the King James Version (KJV) – *public domain*.

ISBN-13: 978-1-6628-1782-3
Ebook ISBN-13: 978-1-6628-1783-0

Table of Contents

Introduction ix
Section One
    The True Nature of Man 1
Section Two
    The Nature and Works of the Flesh 23
Section Three
    Subduing the Flesh 39
Section Four
    Message to the Unbelieving 65

Introduction

*I*magine a world where all human beings lived in peace, joy, and contentment with all that we have, worshipping one God. Imagine having the ability to live with one another in peace despite our differences, without the thoughts of oppression, segregation, and condemnation. Imagine nations free of crime, persecution, and nuclear weapons; just love (divine love) that comes from a pure heart, genuinely loving and caring for your neighbors and environment. As you come back to the here and now, you'll likely begin asking yourself some questions. Why do nations rage? What is it that bothers or scares us so much? Why do we fear one another? What causes us to think that the next person does not have our best interest at heart? Why are nations fighting against one another? Why are fathers walking out of their homes? Why has abortion become the most critical discussion in our societies? Why are kids rebelling against their parents? Why do we try to find peace and satisfaction in hard substances? Why do we discuss race and sexuality like it is so complex and complicated?

Too many questions with no complete and correct answer. Wrong!

There is a perfect explanation for all of these issues, and if we could follow the only solution, the world would be a better place. The only problem is, it is nearly impossible for the whole world to accept this solution.

The world we live in today is in chaos; the system is at the brink of destruction if it does not change its course. The only solution to this world's problem is the same one that the nations of the world have rejected and turned their backs on. The system creates discriminatory excuses as one large enough to rid the world of this one solution that can lead to man and the land's redemption. As a person who believes in a higher power, I cannot seem to fathom why, amid disaster, you would want to eliminate the one thing that can save the people and restore peace and order to society and humanity.

Let us ask ourselves sincerely, "Why is the world in the state that it is presently in, of chaos, anarchy, and doom?" From my understanding of the Bible's viewpoint, the only answer I can provide to this question is found in the state of our hearts and in our understanding of who we truly are. According to the Holy Book, the heart of man is deceitful above all and desperately wicked, who can know it if not the One who created it (Jer. 17:9). Herein lies the problem of humankind, that wickedness lies in every one of us, so that all we can think of is ourselves: me, myself, and I. Humanity has not understood its nature and how it can work around this nature to become a better version of itself. This is so because there is a part of us that we have not been able to tame and control, or better still, put under subjection.

Studies have shown that all human beings have either one or more weaknesses. No one is perfect, and we all can attest to this truth. The ability to work on these weaknesses or put them under subjection is what makes one man different from another, not necessarily better but different and morally upright. Humanity cannot ignore man's frailty in the discussion of weakness, and the truth is that there is something that we can do about it.

Introduction

The beauty of humankind is that we did not just drop from the skies, but instead, we were created from the unique power, of a Higher Being, also known as the Almighty God. Therefore, through Him, we are capable of achieving anything possible.

Genesis 1:2-12 begins the story of creation:

> *And the earth was without form, and void; and darkness was upon the face of the deep. And the Spirit of God moved upon the face of the waters.*
> *And God said, Let there be light: and there was light. And God saw the light, that it was good: and God divided the light from the darkness.*
> *And God called the light Day, and the darkness he called Night. And the evening and the morning were the first day.*
> *And God said, Let there be a firmament in the midst of the waters, and let it divide the waters from the waters.*
> *And God made the firmament, and divided the waters which were under the firmament from the waters which were above the firmament: and it was so.*
> *And God called the firmament Heaven. And the evening and the morning were the second day.*
> *And God said, Let the waters under the heaven be gathered together unto one place, and let the dry land appear: and it was so.*
> *And God called the dry land Earth; and the gathering together of the waters called the Seas: and God saw that it was good.*
> *And God said, Let the earth bring forth grass, the herb yielding seed, and the fruit tree yielding fruit*

> *after his kind, whose seed is in itself, upon the earth: and it was so.*
> *And the earth brought forth grass, and herb yielding seed after his kind, and the tree yielding fruit, whose seed was in itself, after his kind: and God saw that it was good.*
> It goes on to say, in verse 22, that God created the animals, birds of the air, fish of the sea, and He blessed them saying, "Be fruitful and multiply and fill the waters in the seas and let birds multiply on the earth."

It is important that we take notice of God's blessing over the animals, because it is crucial for us to understand what has gone wrong in our world today.

It is pertinent to note how important and valuable the human species is to God, and that He created everything man would need to prosper on earth before considering actually making man. In Genesis 1:26, the Bible states that God said, "Let us make man in our image, after our likeness: and let them have dominion over the fish of the sea, and over the fowl of the air, and over the cattle, and over all the earth, and over every creeping thing that creepeth upon the earth".

Understand this important fact that God created man in His image, in the image of God created He them; male and female He created them. And God blessed them, and God said unto them, "Be fruitful, and multiply, and replenish the earth, and subdue it: and have dominion over the fish of the sea, and over the fowl of the air, and over every living thing that moveth upon the earth". With this knowledge of God's intention for man, it can be understood clearly at this point that we are loved and cherished by this Heavenly Being who thought it wise and necessary to make humans be just like Him. It is safe to say that since we are created in His image, whatever He is, we are as His creation.

So why is the world struggling so hard to kick this great God out of our system?

The first answer to this question is the presence of an age-long enemy, who used to be known as Lucifer but eventually became Satan, also called the Devil, because of his rebellion against Almighty God.

> *And the great dragon was cast out, that old serpent, called the Devil, and Satan, which deceiveth the whole world: he was cast out into the earth, and his angels were cast out with him.*
>
> Rev. 12:9 (KJV)
>
> *And I saw an angel come down from heaven, having the key of the bottomless pit and a great chain in his hand.*
>
> *And he laid hold on the dragon, that old serpent, which is the Devil, and Satan, and bound him a thousand years*
>
> Rev. 20:1-2 (KJV)

This Satan is the enemy of God and his children. He is responsible for the disaster in the world's system today, but the people of the world choose not to see it because they do not see him.

> *Satan, who is the god of this world, has blinded the minds of those who don't believe. They are unable*

> to see the glorious light of the Good News. They don't understand this message about the glory of Christ, who is the exact likeness of God.
>
> 2 Cor. 4:4 (NLT)

In light of this discussion, we can say that man is made up of his strengths and weaknesses. In other words, man's authentic self is who and what he can control and what he allows to take possession of his mind. I am a product of my thought process, and whatever I give my thoughts to becomes the essence of my being.

Bearing in mind that there is a weakness in every human being, in my opinion, it becomes the work of the enemy to feed our weaknesses, making it exceedingly difficult for us to be consistently stable and robust.

One day as I was studying, I remember hearing the Lord speak these words to me: "Satan feeds your ego." If we focus on the literal meaning of the word *ego*, we discover that it solely has a lot to do with self: self-esteem, self-worth, self-respect, self-image, and more. Notice the contrast. We are created in God's image to be more like Him, but according to this statement I heard from God, Satan wants us to be more like ourselves. Remember that we are made from the dust of the earth, thereby making us earthen vessels full of imperfection. So, the more we strive to live according to our true nature, the more imperfect we become. Focusing on our weakness is why we frequently hear people talking about "their truth", which in simple terms means, their struggle.

> Now the serpent was more subtle than any beast of the field which the Lord God had made. And he

said unto the woman, Yea, hath God said, Ye shall not eat of every tree of the garden?

And the woman said unto the serpent, we may eat of the fruit of the trees of the garden:

But of the fruit of the tree which is in the midst of the garden, God hath said, Ye shall not eat of it, neither shall ye touch it, lest ye die.

And the serpent said unto the woman, Ye shall not surely die:

For God doth know that in the day ye eat thereof, then your eyes shall be opened, and ye shall be as gods, knowing good and evil.

And when the woman saw that the tree was good for food, and that it was pleasant to the eyes, and a tree to be desired to make one wise, she took of the fruit thereof, and did eat, and gave also unto her husband with her; and he did eat.

Gen. 3:1-7 (KJV)

When man fell, he lost two precious things. First, was his innocence.

Then the Lord God said, "Behold, the man has become like one of Us, to know good and evil. And now, lest he put out his hand and take also of the tree of life and eat and live forever"

The Mastery of Subduing the Flesh

Gen. 3:22 (KJV)

Second, man lost his authority. God had given man dominion over all He had created, but when man sinned, God said to him,

> *Cursed is the ground for thy sake; in sorrow shalt thou eat of it all the days of thy life;*
>
> *Thorns also and thistles shall it bring forth to thee; and thou shalt eat the herb of the field;*
>
> *In the sweat of thy face shalt thou eat bread, till thou return unto the ground; for out of it wast thou taken: for dust thou art, and unto dust shalt thou return.*

Gen. 3:17-19 KJV)

The fall of man resulted in a loss of true identity, and humanity became deficient in the understanding of who, and Whose, we are. Due to the presence of an unruly enemy on earth, there is a veil that has covered our sight, making it almost impossible for mankind to fathom what exactly is going on behind the scenes of our everyday lives.

SECTION ONE

The True Nature of Man

Man was created by God Almighty in His image and likeness with His breath inside of us. To be made in the image of God is to look like God on both the outside and inside; physically, intellectually, emotionally, and beyond. In all aspects of our being, we are to be like our Creator. If God says we are like Him, isn't it wise to study who He is and to be like Him?

All Scripture is inspired by God, and given to us as our ultimate source of insight and revelation of who He truly is.

Man did not merely fall out of the sky, or evolve from some other animal species into human beings, even if some scientific theories may like to analyze the existence of humanity in this way. God created man, declared that we are good, and gave us charge over everything else that He made. This means that when God created you, He did not just abandon you to figure out who you are all by yourself. Understanding who you are is to understand God's personality and attributes. The greater grasp you have of God, the more you will truly understand who you are, your unique capabilities, and your true purpose. A key part of knowing God is to know that we also have the Holy Spirit's assistance in these matters. Jesus said before he ascended into

Heaven that he would be sending the Holy Spirit to guide us into all truth (John 14:26); this was why it was expedient for Him to return to the Father.

The number one command of the Father to us, His kids, is to remain in a state of holiness because this is His true nature. As God is holy, we also must seek and strive to be holy.

Therefore, the true nature of man is the true nature of God. Discover God, and you discover you.

> *And ye shall be holy unto me: for I the Lord am holy, and have severed you from other people, that ye should be mine.*
>
> Lev. 20:26 (KJV)
>
> *Sanctify yourselves therefore, and be ye holy: for I am the Lord your God.*
>
> Lev. 20:7 (KJV)
>
> *But as he which hath called you is holy, so be ye holy in all manner of conversation;*
>
> *Because it is written, "Be ye holy; for I am holy".*
>
> 1 Peter 1:15-16 (KJV)

Because God created us, this makes Him our one true Master, whom would lead us in the way that He wants us to go. But the enemy came and deceived man, and man, in turn, fell for the lie of the unemployed cherub, Satan.

To properly understand man's true nature, there are two crucial pieces of information that we have to focus on: man's creation and man's restoration.

The Creation of Man

> *And God said, "Let us make man in our image, after our likeness: and let them have dominion over the fish of the sea, and over the fowl of the air, and over the cattle, and over all the earth, and over every creeping thing that creepeth upon the earth". So God created man in his own image, in the image of God created he him; male and female created he them.*
>
> *And God blessed them, and God said unto them, "Be fruitful, and multiply, and replenish the earth, and subdue it: and have dominion over the fish of the sea, and over the fowl of the air, and over every living thing that moveth upon the earth".*
>
> Gen. 1:26-28 (KJV)
>
> *Male and female created he them; and blessed them, and called their name Adam, in the day when they were created.*
>
> Gen. 5:2 (KJV)

Man was created in the image and likeness of God. What exactly does *image* mean?

According to the Google dictionary, an image is a "representation of the external form of a person or thing". Also, "a general impression that a person presents", or "a person or thing that closely resembles another". Additionally, we also have to put the word *likeness* into consideration because we cannot simply say that we physically and externally look like God without considering who we are on the inside.

God's image and likeness within man came from a unique ingredient after God created man from the earth's dust. Adam was nothing more than an object until God breathed life into him. The breath of God made all the difference in man, for it was His BREATH that caused him to truly alive.

> And the Lord God formed man of the dust of the ground, and **breathed** into his nostrils the **breath** of life: and man became a living being.
>
> Gen. 2:7 (KJV)
>
> But there is a spirit within people, the **breath** of the Almighty within them, that makes them intelligent.
>
> Job 32:8 (NLT)

It is this breath of life is the true nature of man. Not our skin or our flesh, but the breath of God that causes us to bear within us the heart of God. This is why God has commanded us all on what to do and what not to do, because He knows that as long as we look up to Him, obey and trust Him, we are enabled and empowered to do as He originally intended for us to dominate the earth with His goodness and power With unconditional love, God Almighty took His time to create earthen vessels into His own physical image, then breathed His own life into us so that we could be like Him on the inside as well. This is why our flesh decays and really should not account for much in determining who we indeed are, but the breath and life of God in us has made man a rarer and more valuable species compared to all the rest of God's creation, because no others were made to bear His image and likeness except for man.

The power of God's breath is illustrated by other authors throughout the Bible. Job said: "By His breath, the heavens are cleared; His hand has pierced the fleeing serpent" (Job 26:13 AMP).

> *If he set his heart upon man, if He gather unto himself his spirit and his breath; All flesh shall perish together, and man shall turn again unto dust.*
>
> Job 34:14-15 (KJV)
>
> King David stated, "By the word of the Lord were the heavens made; and all the host of them by the breath of his mouth" (Ps. 33:6 KJV).
>
> Is it becoming clear how powerful the breath of the Father is within us? You carry the spirit of the Almighty within you. Yet without understanding, we consider ourselves as nothing. The breath of God within us makes us more excellent than the unruly one who moves around like a roaring lion seeking whom he may devour. (1 Peter 5:8).

You are created by God who is seated on the throne of Heaven, and makes the earth His footstool; therefore, we are of God and have overcome this world because He who is in you is greater than he who is in the world.

> *Ye are of God, little children, and have overcome them: because greater is he that is in you, than he that is in the world.*
>
> 1 John 4:4 (KJV)

When man gave in to the serpent's deceit, a gap was created, which caused a change in the communion and communication between God and man. God was present with Adam in the garden, they had a close, intimate relationship, and it was clear to Adam who God was when he had communion with his Father in the cool of the day. But when the old serpent came and Eve was deceived into eating the fruit from the tree of knowledge of good and evil, she then encouraged her husband to do the same. He ate the fruit of the tree that God told them not to eat. Adam listened to the voice of God always and adhered to every instruction God had given him in the garden. He did not know anything apart from what God had told and taught him. However, as soon as Adam ate the apple, all of mankind lost its place before God and earth, giving Satan access to his authority and all that the Father had bestowed upon mankind.

> *And they heard the voice of the Lord God walking in the garden in the cool of the day: and Adam and his wife hid themselves from the presence of the Lord God amongst the trees of the garden.*
>
> Gen. 3:8 (KJV)

After man sinned, he began hiding from God. And so it still is even today that Satan continues to deceive God's children, causing them to hide from their Creator, our one and only true Master. The pattern continues, that we inevitably do something wrong and receive a conviction in our hearts by the power of the Spirit of God, to repent and turn from our wicked and evil ways. Then the old serpent comes to convince us with his schemes and lies, that we cannot be forgiven, just as he was never forgiven, and would have us believe that like him, we must forever be banished from the presence of God. The only answer for us is to fully know and understand the truth that as His sons and daughters God is always able and willing to forgive us God created man in His image, fully empowered and equipped to defeat the enemy.

The Restoration of Man

But there is a great difference between Adam's sin and God's gracious gift. For the sin of this one man, Adam, brought death to many. But even greater is God's wonderful grace and his gift of forgiveness to many through this other man, Jesus Christ. And the result of God's gracious gift is very different from the result of that one man's sin. For Adam's sin led to condemnation, but God's free gift leads to our being made right with God, even though we are guilty of many sins.

Rom. 5:15-16 (NLT)

As we have previously established, the result of Adam eating the fruit was the loss of easy and proper communication with God. As we study the Word of God, we realize that some kind of blood sacrifice to God would be the requirement before God could communicate with them during the days of old. It may not have been written in the Bible that Adam offered any sacrifices to God, but the Bible informed us that his sons Cain and Abel offered sacrifices of the fruit of the ground and the firstborn of his flock and fat. Children do what their parents teach them, so if Cain and Abel offered sacrifices as a practice to worship God, it means it was an act taught to them by their father, Adam. Cain is a perfect example of a man who followed his ego, refusing to accept and obey God's counsel concerning his sacrifice to Him. Instead of adhering to the Almighty God's instruction, he acted upon his weakness, which caused him to take his brother Abel's life.

Following the fall of man in the Garden of Eden and Cain's sin of murder, it seemed as though evil began to increase in the hearts of men. Due to the level of depravity in the world, God began to look for someone who would stay pure so that He could communicate with and represent the people.

> *The Lord observed the extent of human wickedness on the earth, and he saw that everything they thought or imagined was consistently and totally evil.*
>
> Gen. 6:5 (NLT)

Before Moses is eventually chosen to lead the children of Israel out of the land of Egypt, Noah and Enoch were people who walked with God diligently, and He spoke to them directly just as He had Cain and Abel.

> *These are the generations of Noah: Noah was a **just** man and **perfect** in his generations, and **Noah walked with God.***

Take note of Noah's life, the most important information recorded from God's perspective of Noah's life is that he was just, righteous and the fact that he walked with God, fellowshipping diligently with the Lord.

Gen. 6:9 (KJV)

And all the days of Enoch were three hundred sixty and five years:

And Enoch walked with God: *and he was not; for God took him.*

Gen. 5:23-24 (KJV)

The same testament was recorded of Enoch, that he walked diligently with God until the Lord took him.

Through Moses, the law was created. So, the children of Israel had laid down rules from God set on stone to guide them in judging right from wrong. Due to the condition of man's heart, there was a restraint in the communication and relationship between God and man, so He chose prophets who became a medium (like a middle man) between Him and the people. Although God tried talking to the children of Israel face-to-face as He had done with Moses and those before him, they were sore afraid and could not stand the presence of God. So, they requested that Moses continued to talk to God, and he, in turn, would deliver God's message to them.

And all the people saw the thundering, and the lightnings, and the noise of the trumpet, and the mountain smoking: and when the people saw it, they removed, and stood afar off.

> *And they said unto Moses, "Speak thou with us, and we will hear: but let not God speak with us, lest we die".*
>
> *And Moses said unto the people, Fear not: for God is come to prove you, and that his fear may be before your faces, that ye sin not".*
>
> Exod. 20:18 – 21 (KJV)

From the verse above, we clearly see that Moses was not afraid of God's presence, because he had walked closely with God and knew God on a personal and profound level, which had allowed him to have several encounters with God. God revealed Himself to Moses the same way He tried to manifest Himself to Israel's children even though it was through the Burning bush (a different method). The revelation of God makes all the difference.

Initially, Moses was responsible for offering sacrifices to God on behalf of the Israelites, until God chose the Levites to serve as priests in the Tent of Meeting, to assist the people with the offering of these sacrifices to Him. These sacrifices helped to bridge the gap, to a certain extent, between God and the people, but He still did not speak to the children of Israel directly. Some of the sacrifices offered were the whole burnt offering, grain offering, peace offering (also known as slaughter offering), sin offering (also known as the Absolution offering), and guilt offering (sometimes referred to as the compensation offering).

Whole Burnt Offering (Leviticus 1):

This offering was made for the atonement of man. It required **a male herd or flock without blemish or defect,** and whoever brought this animal as an offering **must offer it willingly.** The priests did not have any share of this offering; all of it was given to God, including the blood. The animal had to be washed clean, wood laid out properly on the altar, and the priest would burn it all to God as a pleasing fragrance.

Grain Offering (Leviticus 2):

The grain offering was offered as a form of worship and devotion to the Lord because it had to be offered in memorial of God's deeds for man. It is also known as a thanksgiving offering. The grain offering is one that the people were allowed to prepare by themselves by cooking, but were instructed to avoid using yeast or honey for the unleavened bread, wafer, or cake. The priests were permitted to share from this offering even though it was the most expensive because they had to use fine flour, pour oil on it, and incense it.

Peace Offering (Leviticus 3):

The peace offering is also known as the slaughter offering and is a sacrifice of friendship. This sacrifice restores the covenant of friendship, expressing community between God and the people, and the people themselves. This offering is offered with a **lamb, sheep, or goat without blemish or defect** and is presented alongside the whole burnt offering, and the priests did not partake of this offering.

Sin Offering (Leviticus 4):

The sin offering is also known as the absolution offering. It is offered when a person sins intentionally by straying from any of God's commands, breaking what must not be broken. An absolution offering was provided to God as a **bull without defect or blemish**. The bull was brought to the Tent of Meeting entrance in the presence of God, the individual who has sinned lays his hand on the bull before God. The priest takes some of the bull's blood, brings it into the Tent of Meeting, and he is to pour the rest of the bull's blood out at the base of the Altar of the whole burnt offering at the entrance of the Tent of Meeting.

This offering cannot be offered alone. Like the peace offering, it is offered alongside the whole burnt offering.

Guilt Offering (Leviticus 5):

The guilt offering is also known as the compensation offering. When a person betrays trust and unknowingly sins by straying against any of the holy things of God, he is to bring as his penalty to God, a **ram without defect** from the flock. Alternatively, he may buy one of equal value with silver, as measured by the sanctuary shekel's weight, for a compensation offering. This sacrifice is offered up for a sin you are unaware of. Although it was unintentional, you are guilty before God, hence the guilt offering.

Before the death and resurrection of Christ, there had always been the offering of blood sacrifices, which was required for reconciliation between God and man. Still, the permanent solution to the fall of man was the death of **his** kind without defect or blemish, a man who would give himself up willingly for his friends. The redemption of man was impossible without the spilling of blood because God Himself made it so, if we remember back to the verse in Genesis about the seed and the fruit. The seed can only produce its kind, meaning it is impossible for the blood of animals to redeem mankind, it had to be the blood of a man. The blood of animals could only satisfy or please the Lord for a short period of time, but the ultimate sacrifice required was the blood of a man, for the sake of mankind

> For the **life of the flesh is in the blood**: and I have given it to you upon the altar to make an atonement for your souls: for it is the blood that maketh an atonement for the soul.
>
> Levi. 17:11 (KJV)

> *Greater love hath no man than this that a man lay down his life for his friends.*

John 15 :13 (KJV)

All of these sacrifices and offerings point to the bigger plan that God had for the world. Man, continually offered sacrifices for sins committed knowingly or unknowingly, but God had a greater plan. He had prepared the ultimate sacrifice. Just as it was that sin came into the world by one man, God knew the ultimate sacrifice would require the blood of a man to atone for the mistake of mankind. This promise was stated in the beginning when God cursed the serpent saying,

> "Because you have done this,
> You *are* cursed more than all cattle,
> And more than every beast of the field;
> On your belly, you shall go,
> And you shall eat dust
> All the days of your life.
> And I will put enmity
> Between you and the woman,
> And between your *seed* and her *Seed*;
> He shall bruise your head,
> And you shall bruise His heel. (Gen. 3:14-15 NKJV)

The Seed that God referred to was that ultimate sacrifice which would bruise the head of Satan. This Seed was spoken of by the prophets of old, Abraham saw Him when God asked him to sacrifice his son, Isaac, and David understood this when the Lord showed him several revelations concerning the King to come.

> *The Lord said unto my Lord, sit thou at my right hand until I make Thine enemies thy footstool.*
>
> Ps. 110:1 (KJV)

> *Moses spoke of Him when he said, "I will raise up for them a Prophet like you from among their brethren and will put my words in His mouth, and He shall speak to them all that I command Him. And it shall be that whoever will not hear My word, which He speaks in my name, I will require it of him."*
>
> Deut. 18:15-16 (KJV)

> **He** *indeed was* **foreordained before the foundation of the world.** *Still, He was made manifest in these last times for you, who through Him believe in God, who raised Him from the dead and gave Him glory, so that your faith and hope are in God.* 1 Peter 1:20-21 (NKJV)

> *And all that dwell upon the earth shall worship him, whose names are not written in the book of life of the Lamb slain from the foundation of the world.*
>
> Rev. 13:8 (KJV)

Jesus Christ was prepared for death from the foundation of the world. His coming to earth to die for us was not an afterthought by God, but a premeditated solution before the earth's foundations for man's disobedience. Think about it this way, the Father, Son, and the Holy Spirit came together. They said,

"Before we create man let us establish a solution for any mishap, seeing that we will be creating a being to be like us, but with free will (one who would have the ability to choose and make his own decisions and choices as well as living in a dimension different from ours), who might turn against us (as Lucifer did). It was decided before the creation of the earth began that Jesus Christ, the Son of the Living God, will surrender Himself as the sacrificial lamb, before the creation of the world. All that is in it was created, keeping in mind that all things were created for the enjoyment and benefits of man. This is an assurance to God's children that nothing takes God by surprise. He is very much aware of what is going on and has proffered a solution. We may not fully understand it, and we also do not know how His solution will work, but realize that it is not our purpose or responsibility to know God without the help of the Holy Spirit. It is, however, within our purpose and responsibility to trust Him, always. The scriptures have shown us, He is the Sovereign God. He sees all things, knows all things, and is everywhere at the same time. Absolutely nothing is hidden from Him. In all His Sovereignty, God would not allow man's sin in the garden to take Him by surprise. So, from the beginning, Jesus Christ was prepared as a sacrifice being led to slaughter for the propitiation of our sins.

The prophet Isaiah said it this way, in Isaiah 53:7,

"He was oppressed, and he was afflicted, yet he opened not his mouth: he is brought as a lamb to the slaughter, and as a sheep before her shearers is dumb, so he openeth not his mouth."

The beautiful thing about this lamb is that He is the Son of God; the Bible records Him as a King, Savior, and Messiah who was coming to save the world.

> *For unto us a child is born, unto us a son is given: and the government shall be upon his shoulder: and his name shall be called Wonderful, Counsellor, The mighty God, The everlasting Father, The Prince of Peace.*
>
> *Of the increase of his government and peace there shall be no end, upon the throne of David, and upon his kingdom, to order it, and to establish it with judgment and with justice from henceforth even forever. The zeal of the Lord of hosts will perform this.*
>
> Isa. 9:6-7(KJV)

Therefore, Jesus Christ was sent to the world to restore man unto himself, according to God's original plan, that is having a deep and personal relationship with Him. As a result, God will never ask any man to offer any blood sacrifices to Him again. No one ever again has to sacrifice their children, animals, or other persons as a ransom for sin, because the ultimate sacrifice was given to us the day Jesus Christ was beaten, oppressed, afflicted, and finally crucified on the cross. History has shown that in those days one of the worst methods of death was the crucifixion on a cross and according to the Scriptures cursed is the man who hangs on a tree (Galatians 3:13).

Crucifixion is a method of punishment or capital punishment in which the victim is tied or nailed to a large wooden beam and left to hang perhaps for several days, until eventual death from exhaustion and asphyxiation. (culled from Wikipedia, October 2019)

> *Christ hath redeemed us from the curse of the law,*
> *being made a curse for us: for it is written, Cursed*
> *is every one that hangeth on a tree: (Galatians 3:13)*

It is no wonder that Jesus Christ, living in flesh as a man, cried to his father, praying that this cup would pass from him ... but that not His will, but the will of the Father, should be done (Matt. 26:39). The Lord was also hurting deeply, knowing that his Father, and the Holy Spirit who was in him, would depart from him. The thought of this made him weary, as the Psalmist said in Psalm 51:11-12,

"Cast me not away from thy presence; and take not thy holy spirit from me.

Restore unto me the joy of thy salvation; and uphold me with thy free spirit."

This was the pain of Jesus Christ being crucified on the cross; His Father turned His face away from him, because even though he himself was without sin, like the lamb without defect or blemish Jesus Christ himself became sin. He was a substitution for us, and his Father could not behold Him on the cross.

> *And he went a little farther, and fell on his face, and*
> *prayed, saying, O my Father, if it be possible, let*
> *this cup pass from me: nevertheless, not as I will,*
> *but as thou wilt.*
>
> *Three times our Lord and Savior said this prayer*
> *in great despair and sorrow. Jesus Christ knew*
> *very well what He was getting into but He did not*
> *defend Himself in any way, He chose to be guilty*
> *because we are indeed guilty. By His death we were*
> *made innocent before God, we were justified by*
> *the blood of the Lamb, we were given a new and*

> *living hope, that in the resurrection of Christ we all have become a new creation.*

Matt. 26:39 (KJV)

> *Blessed be the God and Father of our Lord Jesus Christ, which according to his abundant mercy hath begotten us again unto a lively hope by the resurrection of Jesus Christ from the dead.*

1 Peter 1:3 (KJV)

> *Therefore, if any man be in Christ, he is a new creature: old things are passed away; behold, all things are become new.*

2 Cor. 5:17 (KJV)

> *For God so loved the world, that he gave his only begotten Son, that whosoever believeth in him should not perish, but have everlasting life.*

John 3:16 (KJV)

At this point in our lives, it is important to also note that there is no way to know God but through Jesus Christ alone. Jesus Christ is the chosen Seed to bring restoration, redemption, deliverance, and hope to God's children. It is through Him that so many more seeds (in the persons of you and I) have been brought forth to bruise the head of the serpent. With that in mind, there is little wonder why the world keeps advocating for abortion, as the enemy knows that man (who understands his authority in Christ) stands as a threat to his kingdom and agenda.

Redemption does not come from the north, south, east, or west but from God above.

Jesus Christ said "I am the way, the truth, and the life. No one comes to the Father except through me." (John 14:6 KJV)

In addition to our salvation through the sacrifice of Jesus Christ we have also regained our authority as children of God. The name of Jesus Christ carries all the authority in both heaven and earth. He commanded us to ask anything (according to the will of the Father) in His name so that the Father will be glorified.

> *And whatever you ask in My name, that I will do, that the Father may be glorified in the Son. If you ask anything in My name, I will do it.*

John 14:13-14 (KJV)

> *Wherefore God also hath highly exalted him, and given him a name which is above every name:*
> *That at the name of Jesus every knee should bow, of things in heaven, and things in earth, and things under the earth;*
> *And that every tongue should confess that Jesus Christ is Lord, to the glory of God the Father.*

Phil. 2:9-11 (KJV)

Through the blood of one man alone are we restored and redeemed unto the Father, and in Him we enjoy the same relationship Adam did with God in the beginning, in the Garden of Eden. Now we can walk with God just like Abraham, Noah, Enoch, Moses, and Apostle Paul, because of Christ's sacrifice on the cross.

As important as the offerings of old were, the Lord stated,

> "This is what the Lord of Heaven's Armies, the God of Israel, says: "Take your burnt offerings and your other sacrifices and eat them yourselves! When I led your ancestors out of Egypt, it was not burnt offerings and sacrifices I wanted from them. This is what I told them: 'Obey me, and I will be your God, and you will be my people. Do everything as I say, and all will be well!'
>
> Samuel also said the same thing to King Saul when he said "obedience is better than sacrifice".
>
> Jer. 7:23 (NLT)
>
> But Samuel replied: "Does the Lord delight in burnt offerings and sacrifices as much as in obeying the Lord? To obey is better than sacrifice, and to heed is better than the fat of rams.
>
> 1 Sam.15:22 (NIV)

When God says anything, it becomes law, and no one can change that. The Lord wanted His people to hear His voice and obey His words. In John 1 we are told that "the Word of God was made flesh and it dwelt among men". This implies that right now the Word of God is our redemption, which is in the person of Jesus Christ. In the days of old, the children of Israel rejected the Word of God, though He kept speaking and telling them how important His commands were. They preferred to do evil, though, and then offer sacrifices to God for forgiveness and atonement. But the Lord specifically requests obedience to His Word more than anything else. This is why, after the death and resurrection of Jesus Christ (the Word of God personified), we are instructed to accept Him as our Lord and Savior. However, we are currently rejecting Him, just like the Israelites in the days of old.

> *In the beginning was the Word and the Word was with God and the Word was God.*
>
> John 1:1 (NIV)
>
> *For whosoever shall call upon the name of the Lord shall be saved.*
>
> Rom. 10:13 (KJV)
>
> *For thou desirest not sacrifice; else would I give it: thou delightest not in burnt offering.*
>
> *The sacrifices of God are a broken spirit: a broken and a contrite heart, O God, thou wilt not despise.*
>
> Ps. 51:16-17 (KJV)

King David also understood that to genuinely touch God one must repent from the heart. No child of God is obligated to offer any sacrifice to God except the sacrifice of praise. No blood offering is either requested or accepted. Therefore, we must never offer any blood sacrifices to anything or anyone in the name of atonement and redemption, because the ultimate sacrifice has been given by God Himself. This is the only sacrifice that restored man to His original position with God.

SECTION TWO

The Nature and Works of the Flesh

"The flesh", in simple terms, represents the carnal nature of man. This is the physical part of man which causes man to have desires for things in addition to what is actually needed to sustain life. It is the "humus" (meaning dust) part of man, which is in constant conflict with the spirit. The Bible also refers to the flesh as the sinful nature of man that causes him to be disobedient to the laws of the Lord. The issue with the flesh is that it constantly demands its satisfaction, and without Christ, there exists a restlessness if its desires are not granted. The flesh is also the body that we see, which can also be referred to as our mortal body; the part of us that can die. Apostle Paul said that it was because of the flesh that the things he did not want to do he found himself doing.

> I do not understand what I do. For what I want to do I do not do, but what I hate I do.
>
> Rom. 7:15(NIV)

An amazing thing about the flesh is that it does not change or repent. It is what it is. It likes what it likes and it wants what it wants, and only God understands this. Think, for a moment, of what happened in the beginning. God formed man from the 'dust' of the earth. This means man was formed out of the earth; therefore, our physical nature is of the earth. In other words, the flesh can only receive satisfaction from earthly things, and this further confirms that there is nothing spiritual about the flesh. It desires the things that the earth has to offer, which can also be referred to as worldly pleasures. When the flesh is provided with all that it desires; food, drinks of all kinds, sex, etc., we would consider ourselves to have reached a state of happiness. This type of happiness, however, does not in any way relate to the joy that is from the Holy Ghost, according to Galatians 5:22, which tells us that joy is one of the fruits of the Spirit.

Since we know that the spirit of man is the breath of God in us, and the flesh is the dust of the earth, we can now grasp that the flesh cannot carry out spiritual activities if it has not been made subject to the things of the spirit. Apostle Paul stated that as soon as the law was created the body came to the knowledge of what it was and constantly disobeyed the law. The carnal nature of man causes man to be in constant disobedience to laws and authorities set above us. If not for the ten commandments, according to the book of Romans, the sinful nature of man would not have been able to tell right from wrong. The law showed man the correct path, and this made it all the more difficult for the carnal man to obey. This is the nature of our flesh.

> *What shall we say then? Is the law sin? God forbid. Nay, I had not known sin, but by the law: for I had not known lust, except the law had said, thou shalt not covet.*
>
> Rom. 7:7 (KJV)

The Nature And Works Of The Flesh

This should provide clarity as to why Satan tempts us with the things of the flesh and constantly uses those things to distract us from our journey with Jesus Christ. Food is good, but too much of it becomes gluttony, which can cause a distraction for the spirit being that lives within you. Wealth is good, but what you may become while in possession of wealth becomes the issue. Love and affection are beautiful within the confines of marriage, but the flesh may tell you it is not just limited to marriage, or gender, or that there is no age restriction.

It is commonly believed that the flesh is weak. The Bible attests to this in Matthew 26:41 (KJV), "Watch and pray, that ye enter not into temptation: the spirit indeed is willing, but the flesh is weak." This implies that if we allow the flesh to succeed over us, and both spirit and flesh become weak, this will displease the Lord, and we shall have no place with Him. The Bible states in John 4:23-24 (KJV), "But the hour cometh, and now is, when the true worshippers shall worship the Father in spirit and in truth: for the Father seeketh such to worship him.

God is a Spirit: and they that worship him must worship him in spirit and in truth."

As human beings, if the flesh is not put under submission very quickly it can become a problem for one's self as well as for generations to come. It can cause God to look or turn away from you. The flesh wants what it wants, and if it is continually fed what it desires this will eventually cause destruction to the spirit man. Summing it up, the more you feed your flesh, your spirit man is subdued, or put under subjection to your flesh, which is appeasing to the enemy. For he is the one who continues to provoke in us unnecessary cravings, even as we think it is simply our bodies desiring something nice, which looks or feels good.

> *You say, "I am allowed to do anything"-but not everything is good for you. You say, "I am allowed to do anything"-but not everything is beneficial.*
>
> 1 Cor. 10:23 (NLT)

Apostle Paul is stating clearly that not everything the flesh wants is beneficial. We live in a world, today, where people state that they are what they are and there is nothing that can be done about it, but this is not so, because if there is anything that God has blessed man with the ability to do, it is the ability to change.

> *And be not conformed to this world: but be ye transformed by the renewing of your mind, that ye may prove what is that good, and acceptable, and perfect, will of God.*
>
> Rom. 12:2 (KJV)

The Lord has given unto us the spirit of transformation through the renewing of our minds. because we are indeed carnally minded. The reason we are given the ability to change is for the perfect will of God to be done. Any man can change. How? By subduing the flesh, which means putting the flesh in submission to your spirit by allowing the spirit to be in control of your desires. For when you allow your spirit to be in control it means that the Spirit of our Lord and Savior Jesus Christ has found His place in you and has begun its work in you.

Unfortunately, living life as it pleases you will only lead to death, and after that, you have to face God. This will not be a matter of choice, but just what is. This is why the Bible admonishes us in Galatians 5:16 (KJV), "This I say then, 'Walk in the Spirit, and ye shall not fulfil the lust of the flesh'."

Continually fulfilling the desires of the flesh leads to sin, which leads to death.

> *For the wages of sin is death; but the gift of God is eternal life through Jesus Christ our Lord.*
>
> Rom. 6:23 (KJV)

Driving Force of the Flesh

The major force that drives the flesh is desire. Some of us might call it craving. The flesh always has a need for something, it is in constant want, and if not checked we will feed it to our very own destruction. The Bible tells us about three major methods by which the flesh makes its demands, according to 1 John 2.

Love not the world, neither the things that are in the world. If any man loves the world, the love of the Father is not in him.

> *For all that is in the world, the lust of the flesh, and the lust of the eyes, and the pride of life, is not of the Father, but is of the world.*
>
> 1 John 2:15-17 (KJV)

Lust of the flesh

The desire for the basic things of life, for survival, in and of itself is not a bad thing. The basic essentials for life are food, water, shelter, general comfort, and for an adult, sex. It is the excessive desire for these things that can lead to death. For example, too much food leads to gluttony, which leads to obesity, which can eventually result in death in the form of high blood pressure, diabetes, breathing disorders, heart problems, just to mention a few. It is good to desire shelter, but when this desire shifts from obtaining a place to lay your head, to doing anything, at all costs, to build mansions, or to gain far more than is actually required for safety and security. This path also becomes dangerous. It can be stated at this point that when any singular good thing becomes an addiction, then it is something you need to watch out for.

Remember that the essential purpose of the body is to house the Spirit of God to allow Him to operate within us here on earth. Hence, the Lord's prayer:

> *After this manner therefore pray ye: Our Father which art in heaven, Hallowed be thy name.*
> *Thy kingdom come, Thy will be done in earth, as it is in heaven.*
>
> Matt. 6:9-10 (KJV)

The only way God's will can be established here on earth, and within us, is when we allow the Spirit to abide in a body that is not controlled by our sinful nature, thereby allowing God to lead us in all totality. This may sound difficult, but Apostle Paul said that the grace of God is sufficient for us in our weakness. He is our strength when we are weak. The Spirit of God identifies a weakness in man and when we call on Him for help, he looks for those weaknesses in us and replaces them with His strength.

> *And he said unto me, My grace is sufficient for thee: for my strength is made perfect in weakness. Most*

The Nature And Works Of The Flesh

gladly therefore will I rather glory in my infirmities, that the power of Christ may rest upon me.

2 Cor. 12:9 (KJV)

Putting the flesh in submission to the Spirit helps us to conquer the desires of the flesh. After all, it is written in Romans 8:11 (KJV),

"But if the Spirit of him that raised up Jesus from the dead dwell in you, he that raised up Christ from the dead shall also **quicken your mortal bodies by his Spirit** that dwelleth in you."

The same power that raised Jesus from the grave lives in us, therefore once we surrender the desires of the flesh to the Spirit, it becomes possible to fulfill the purposes of God.

The lust of the flesh is a major tool that the enemy utilizes to destroy God's children, particularly relating to sex. Unfortunately, sex, as God intended it, has been misunderstood and devalued. We must be careful to remember and understand that sex was created and fashioned by God, not Satan, or by any demon. However, it is the work of our ancient enemy to constantly attempt to make every beautiful thing that God has created into a tool for our destruction. Now sex has been so misunderstood, that we often no longer understand that it was created for the sole purpose of procreation within the confines of marriage. Sex, as created by God, is a beautiful tool used to unite the souls of two people which eventually creates one soul (the child). This is why the Bible says "and two shall become one". In other words, same-sex relationships cannot be the will of the Father because it contradicts His original purpose. Fornication and adultery cannot be the will of God, because they defile the concept of marriage.

God created male and female, but there are now people who were born female claiming to be male, and vice versa.

The Mastery of Subduing the Flesh

There are some who claim the term 'non-binary', meaning that they are neither male nor female. It is important to note at this point that all of this is the spirit of the antichrist at work in God's children. Demons do not have genders and cannot be limited to male and female. With no intention of sounding offensive, any man or woman who claims to be the opposite of whatever they are is possessed by something that they are not aware of. While there are some perfectly good people who claim to be gay, if the Holy Spirit was present in the life of these individuals, He would guide him/her to the truth of God's Word concerning them, as the Bible is not an author of confusion. Demons are merely expressing themselves in these individuals. We are gradually heading to the days of Sodom and Gomorrah when the Lord decided to destroy these two cities with fire. Sexual immorality was rampant and disastrous, so that the angels stated that the Lord had heard the outcry of His people concerning the wickedness in those towns. Almost no one had respect for their bodies, and no one was safe. Everyone would have been destroyed, had it not been for the prayer of Abraham for Lot and his household.

Today, Satan has so blinded God's people, that sex is a tool used for sales in business and movies, as well as a method of promotion within the music industry. It is even used as a weapon, during wars, to abuse and molest women and children.

Understand this: your body is the Lord's sanctuary, and the temple of the Lord. It is the place of dwelling for the Spirit of God, and the enemy understands this. So, he wants you to use it in any and all ways that it would most displease the Lord. Although some people believe that it is a natural desire to want to share a bed with someone of the same sex, or to sleep with a man or woman that you are not married to, I can tell you categorically that it is the spirit of immorality at work. Satan's greatest strategy has always been to make it appear as if he does not exist in our thoughts and minds. Meanwhile, every thought that wells up inside of you that is contrary to the ways and will of God is from the spirit of the antichrist.

The use of hard drugs cannot be omitted, for every time our body is distorted due to the use of some hypnotic substance which, again, was created for positive and healthy consumption, such as prescriptions meant to help relieve pains, we abuse God's sanctuary. Drugs and alcohol, when abused, can cause you to become demon-possessed, immediately resulting in the exit of the Spirit of God from your body.

So, I say, let the Holy Spirit guide your lives. Then you won't be doing what your sinful nature craves. The sinful nature wants to do evil, which is just the opposite of what the Spirit wants. And the Spirit gives us desires that are the opposite of what the sinful nature desires. These two forces are constantly fighting each other, so you are not free to carry out your good intentions. But when you are directed by the Spirit, you are not under obligation to the law of Moses.

> *When you follow the desires of your sinful nature, the results are very clear: sexual immorality, impurity, lustful pleasures, idolatry, sorcery, hostility, quarreling, jealousy, outbursts of anger, selfish ambition, dissension, division, envy, drunkenness, wild parties, and other sins like these. Let me tell you again, as I have before, that anyone living that sort of life will not inherit the Kingdom of God.*
>
> Gal. 5:16-21 (NLT)
>
> *"I have the right to do anything," you say—but not everything is beneficial. "I have the right to do anything"—but I will not be mastered by anything.*

You say, "Food for the stomach and the stomach for food, and God will destroy them both." The body, however, is not meant for sexual immorality but for the Lord, and the Lord for the body. By his power, God raised the Lord from the dead, and he will raise us also. Do you not know that your bodies are members of Christ himself? Shall I then take the members of Christ and unite them with a prostitute? Never! Do you not know that he who unites himself with a prostitute is one with her in body? For it is said, "The two will become one flesh." But whoever is united with the Lord is one with him in spirit. Flee from sexual immorality. All other sins a person commits are outside the body, but whoever sins sexually, sins against their own body. Do you not know that your bodies are temples of the Holy Spirit, who is in you, whom you have received from God? You are not your own; you were bought at a price. Therefore, honor God with your bodies.

1 Cor. 6:12-20 (NLT)

Lust of the eyes

Williams Shakespeare once said that the eye is the window to the soul. I may not fully know what he was trying to say, but as a child of God, this is my interpretation: whatever your eyes look upon plants a seed within your heart. There are certain things we behold with our eyes and we regret ever seeing them. We cannot unsee something because our minds now have the access to play it over and over again.

> *The light of the body is the eye: if therefore thine eye be single; thy whole body shall be full of light. But if thine eye be evil; thy whole body shall be full of darkness. If therefore the light that is in thee be darkness, how great is that darkness!*
>
> Matt. 6:22-23 (KJV)

The lust of the eyes leads to the sin of covetousness, which is to desire someone else's property. Other sins associated with the lust of the eyes have to do with pornography, and visual lust of both men and women, which can give birth to homosexuality, adultery, and fornication.

> *But I say unto you, "That whosoever looketh on a woman to lust after her hath committed adultery with her already in his heart".*
>
> *And if thy right eye offends thee, pluck it out, and cast it from thee: for it is profitable for thee that one of thy members should perish, and not that thy whole body should be cast into hell.*
>
> *And if thy right hand offends thee, cut it off, and cast it from thee: for it is profitable for thee that one of thy members should perish, and not that thy whole body should be cast into hell.*
>
> Matt. 5:28-30 (KJV)
>
> *So, then faith cometh by hearing, and hearing by the word of God.*

Rom. 10:17 (KJV)

If you can prayerfully and carefully sift the things that your eyes see then you will be able to abstain from almost any temptation. Sin starts in the heart, but it only gets to the heart because of what the eyes have seen or what the ears have heard. This is why the kinds of movies we watch and the music we listen to affects us spiritually. People have ruined their destinies by allowing themselves to sit under the anointing of demonic songs and movies, and their lives began to take a turn for the worst. Someone may find themselves desiring things that they had not previously been interested in, and then begin to wonder how all this started. So, it is important to guard your eyes. The more you see things that are not of God, gradually you fall into sin, satisfying the flesh which will eventually lead to death. When it comes to our ears, I remember the Lord telling me that music is prayer. Remember that the Bible states that death and life are in the power of the tongue, and they that love it shall eat the fruit thereof (Proverbs 18:21). There are songs with lyrics which cannot be stated in clear sentences because they are so offensive. I once heard a colleague of mine lip syncing a rap song and I immediately asked him to turn off the music because of the words he was saying. When I asked him to say the words to me, he said he could not do it because it was so unappealing to the ear. Have you ever wondered why you cannot stop using swear words? Check the music that you listen to and the movies you watch. Be careful to sing songs that edify your soul, because you gradually become what you sing! These are some causes of struggle for younger generations. Wrong music, sex-filled movies, idol worship, a do-as-you-please kind of life style, or a mindset that says "I do not care what you do with yourself as long as it does not affect me and it makes you happy". All of these things are destructive. One should maintain their dignity, by keeping their hearing and vision pure.

Pride of Life

Pride of life is a desire for power or for a position of authority. It is also giving glory to yourself for the things that you feel you have accomplished on your own, without God's help, such as a good education, an amazing career or a large business empire.

> I am the vine, ye are the branches: He that abideth in me, and I in him, the same bringeth forth much fruit: **for without me ye can do nothing.**
>
> John 15:5 (KJV)

As human beings, we all desire to receive credit for the good or great things that we have done or are doing. This is not a bad thing on its own. The potential for a problem comes about if that desire is coupled with feelings of superiority or a desire to subdue other people and have them give glory to us. We are no more than earthen vessels, which can drop dead at any time.

Every time I think of pride, I remember the story of Nebuchadnezzar who was turned into a beast because of his pride and arrogance for a kingdom God gave him.

> At the end of twelve months, he walked in the palace of the kingdom of Babylon. The king spake, and said, "Is not this great Babylon, that I have built for the house of the **kingdom by the might of my power, and for the honor of my majesty?"**

> *While the word was in the king's mouth, there fell a voice from heaven, saying, O king Nebuchadnezzar, to thee it is spoken; The kingdom is departed from thee.*
> *And they shall drive thee from men, and thy dwelling shall be with the beasts of the field: they shall make thee to eat grass as oxen, and seven times shall pass over thee, until thou know that the Most High ruleth in the kingdom of men, and giveth it to whomsoever he will.*
>
> Dan. 4:29-32 (KJV)

Pride comes before a fall. We should always be mindful of that and know that self-glorification and vain glory are no different from pride. We may be more intelligent than others, richer than others, or even better looking than others, but we were not made so to intimidate another, but to bring men and women to the kingdom of God in humility. There is nothing that we have, as humans, that was not given to us by God. When God created us, in the beginning, He gave us dominion over the birds of the air, fish of the sea and every creeping thing, He never asked us to dominate other human beings like ourselves, but instead we were admonished to love one another.

> *And God said, "Let us make man in our image, after our likeness: and let them have **dominion over the fish of the sea, and over the fowl of the air, and over the cattle, and over all the earth, and over every creeping thing that creepeth upon the earth.**"*
>
> Gen. 1:26 (KJV)

> *Beloved, let us love one another: for love is of God; and every one that loveth is born of God, and knoweth God.*
>
> 1 John 4:7 (KJV)

It is the enemy who has tempted us with desires for power and dominion over other people, but this is not the will of God. For some of us, this may very well be the reason why God has not prospered us, because He has seen our potential future and how we may intimidate or disrespect others because of the gifts that He has given to us. However, the Lord will not allow His gifts to lead His children into hell.

> *The fear of the Lord is the instruction of wisdom, and before honor is humility.*
>
> Prov. 15:33 (KJV)

God honors those who love and fear Him. This is why He wants us to also love and honor others, and not consider ourselves too highly or better than anyone else.

> *For I say, through the grace given unto me, to every man that is among you, not to think of himself more highly than he ought to think; but to think soberly, according as God hath dealt to every man the measure of faith.*
>
> Rom. 12:3 (KJV)

SECTION THREE

Subduing the Flesh

When God created man in the garden, He wanted us to be innocent and pure in heart, just like little babies not knowing good from evil, right or wrong. God's intention was for us to be like children before Him, taking instructions and directions from Him alone. This is why He commanded Adam in the beginning, saying, "And the Lord God commanded the man, saying, of every tree of the garden thou mayest freely eat: **But of the tree of the knowledge of good and evil, thou shalt not eat of it: for in the day that thou eatest thereof thou shalt surely die.**" (Gen. 2:16-17 KJV)

For a moment, think about a couple who have just become parents, of a cute little baby. The desire of those parents is that the child remains under their wings, obeying the instructions being given to him/her, without showing any form of contempt towards the parent. As parents, because we know that the world is unsafe, we set rules and create boundaries for our kids, advise them on issues pertaining to life in general, and hope that no matter what, our kids will remain on the path that we have set for them, and generally abide by the rules and commands that have been laid down for them.

This was exactly what God had planned for Adam. God created Adam to be like an offspring to Him, and desired to love, care, nurture, guide, lead, and protect Adam like a father would his son. There was no hidden secret to the command that God gave Adam about the tree of knowledge of good and evil. It was exactly what God said it was.

When Eve came along, maybe there was a misunderstanding in the interpretation of God's message from Adam to Eve, because when the serpent (the fallen cherub) came to her, he said, "Has God indeed said, 'You shall not eat of every tree of the garden'?" And the woman said to the serpent, "We may eat the fruit of the trees of the garden; but of the fruit of the tree which is in the midst of the garden, God has said, 'You shall not eat it, nor shall you touch it, lest you die.'" (Gen. 3:1-3 NKJV)

It seems as though Eve had no idea why the fruit of the tree in the midst of the garden should not have been eaten. Besides that, God never said it should not be touched. He said that the fruit of the tree of knowledge of good and evil should not be eaten. As God's children, it is important to carefully listen to God's instructions and follow them to the letter, without care for what anyone else says. In the Bible, there are instructions that the Lord has given to us to guide and transform us into becoming whom He has created us to be, but disobedience will never allow us to attain the level of spirituality and deliverance that He has prepared for us. Always remember that when you have any misunderstanding of God's word or instruction, it is better to go directly to Him to seek clarity. Avoid the counsel of those whose stance on faith, or whose race with Christ, you are unsure of.

This was the mistake Eve made, as she was having a discussion with an entity she really did not know, and inadvertently allowed herself to be deceived. She believed that what she was doing was right, but ultimately influenced Adam to eat the forbidden fruit, as well as herself. This indeed showed the innocence in Eve, and shockingly, the same lie Lucifer used to deceive himself while in heaven he also sold to Eve, and she fell for it.

> The serpent then said to the woman, "You will not surely die. For God knows that in the day you eat of it your eyes will be opened, and **you will be like God**, knowing good and evil."

(Gen. 3:4-5 NKJV)

It is clear that the serpent had more knowledge of the tree than Eve, because the statement of the serpent was partially true. After all, when Adam and Eve ate the fruit, they did not physically die but they died to God. Man lost his place and position before God and God said, "Behold, the man is become as one of us, to know good and evil: and now, lest he put forth his hand, and take also of the tree of life, and eat, and live forever" (Gen. 3:22 NKJV).

As children of God, our success in this race with Christ is dependent on the proper understanding of God's Word. We must prayerfully seek the face of the Lord when we study His Word so that the Holy Spirit can guide and give us understanding so that we are not misled by the enemy.

To fully master the art of subduing the flesh, what happened in the beginning cannot ever be ignored. The story which played out in the Garden of Eden is much the same as the one being played out in our lives presently. There are several points to take note of:

1) Adam was created as a child of God. we are also created to be children of God.

> Jesus Christ said to His disciples "Suffer little children, and forbid them not, to come unto me: for of such is the kingdom of heaven."
>
> Matt. 19:14 KJV
>
> Then Jesus called a little child to Him, set him in the midst of them, and said, "And Jesus called a little child unto him, and set him in the midst of them and said, "Verily I say unto you, except ye be converted, and become as little children, ye shall not enter into the kingdom of heaven.
>
> Matt. 18:2-3 KJV

2) Adam was given authority over everything on earth. We are also given authority over everything on earth, by the power in the death and resurrection of our Lord and Savior Jesus Christ

   > "Behold, I give unto you power to tread on serpents and scorpions, and over all the power of the enemy: and nothing shall by any means hurt you
   >
   > Luke 10:19 KJV

3) Adam walked and talked with God. As God's children today, it is impossible to follow God without walking closely with him, and remaining in constant communication with Him, because it is in the place of prayer that we receive from God.

If you abide in Me, and My words abide in you, you will ask what you desire, and it shall be done for you.

John 15:7 KJV

And hereby we do know that we know him, if we keep his commandments. He that saith, I know him, and keepeth not his commandments, is a liar, and the truth is not in him. But whoso keepeth his word, in him verily is the love of God perfected: hereby know we that we are in him. He that saith he abideth in him ought himself also so to walk, even as he walked.

1 John 2:3-6 KJV

4) Adam disobeyed God, which caused him to lose his benefits from God.

Jesus answered and said unto him, If a man love me, he will keep my words: and my Father will love him, and we will come unto him, and make our abode with him.

John 14:23 KJV

    The life that Jesus lived on earth shows us that it is possible to subdue the flesh and live a holy life. Some might say "But Jesus Christ was God on earth! We are not God, so it is impossible to be perfect." But the Bible is clear, as it commands us to be holy, even as our Lord is holy, meaning it is achievable. (Matt. 5:48)

    With that being said, there are four major steps to consider in order to master the art of subduing the flesh. Bear in mind that none of these are achievable without the assistance of the Holy Spirit, we were not given that ability at all. God created us in such a way that makes it impossible to attain good success without him, this is why we need to humble ourselves before God allow Him perform His wonders in our lives which yields transformation and a renewing of our minds.

Step One: Self-Control

> *But the fruit of the Spirit is love, joy, peace, long-suffering, kindness, goodness, faithfulness, gentleness, **self-control**. Against such there is no law.*
>
> Gal. 5:22-23 (NKJV)

Self-control is the ability to maintain control (which is the power to influence) over oneself, in particular one's emotions and desires, or the expression of them in one's behavior, and especially in difficult situations. In simple terms, it is the ability to constantly keep your emotions, words and character in check. Therefore, it is impossible to speak about subduing the flesh without speaking about self-control. In Galatians, we are told that self-control is one of the nine fruits of the spirit. What does fruit of the spirit mean?

The fruits of the spirit are the attributes that man begins to possess as a result of the work of the Holy Spirit in one's life.

> *But as many as received him, to them gave he **power** to become the sons of God, even to them that believe on his name...*
>
> John 1:12 KJV

So, the King James version says power while the New King James Version says "right":

> But as many as received Him, to them He gave the **right** to become children of God, to those who believe in His name...

John 1:12 NKJV

What does "right" mean?

From a legal perspective, it means "a moral or legal entitlement to have or obtain something or to act in a certain way". When you are entitled to something you have a right to that thing. Entitlement, in this context, means that there are certain privileges that being born again gives you access to, and receiving the Holy Spirit is one of them. The day you accept Jesus Christ as your Lord and Savior, you become a new creation, you are born anew and old things are passed away.

> Therefore, if any man be in Christ, he is a new creature: old things are passed away; behold, all things are become new.

2 Cor. 5:17 KJV

So as a child of God, when you receive Jesus Christ you are entitled to becoming a true son of God, which is why the King James Version states that we receive power to be called the sons of God. How then do we receive power as children of God?

We receive power by the in-filling of the Holy Spirit, just like the disciples on the day of Pentecost, as they met together in the upper room:

> *But you shall receive power when the Holy Spirit has come upon you; and you shall be witnesses to Me in Jerusalem, and in all Judea and Samaria, and to the end of the earth.*
>
> Acts 1:8 KJV
>
> *For as many as are led by the Spirit of God, these are sons of God.*
>
> Rom. 8:14 KJV

Without the Spirit of God at work in our lives we cannot truly be called sons of God. You cannot accept Jesus as your Lord and Savior and ignore the workings of His Spirit. Apostle Paul said:

> *But ye are not in the flesh, but in the Spirit, if so be that the Spirit of God dwell in you. Now if any man have not the Spirit of Christ, he is none of his.*
>
> Rom. 8:9 KJV

This means that much work needs to be done in the life of a believer of Christ. One must submit themselves to the work of the Spirit of God in order to truly live as a Spirit-led child of God.

The Spirit of God, if allowed to operate in our lives, empowers us to become the new creature that 2 Corinthians 5:17 talks about. The Bible states that the Holy Spirit searches all things and guides us into all truth, when we allow the Holy Spirit to search and guide us. He helps us to be more like Christ each day. The effects of the power of the Holy Spirit in our lives is the evidence of the fruits of the Holy Spirit.

Our lives in connection with the Holy Spirit can be likened to the seeds and the fruits which we read about in Genesis. Since we are God's children (His seed) and the Holy Spirit can only yield according to His kind in us, working closely with the Holy Spirit helps us become like the One we ourselves were created from, and we become like a product, or fruit of, the seed that is sown. Fruit is the result or reward of work or activity of the Holy Spirit in our lives. Constant submission to the Holy Spirit births the Christ-likeness in us.

When we see a person, who is like Christ in word and deed, we are witnessing the evidence that this person has given the Holy Spirit access to work and bear fruit in his/her life.

In the Book of Jeremiah chapter 31:31 – 34 (KJV), God said He was coming into a new covenant with His children.

Behold, the days come, saith the Lord, that I will make a new covenant with the house of Israel, and with the house of Judah:

Not according to the covenant that I made with their fathers in the day that I took them by the hand to bring them out of the land of Egypt; which my covenant they brake, although I was a husband unto them, saith the Lord:

But this shall be the covenant that I will make with the house of Israel; After those days, saith the Lord, I will put my law in their inward parts, and write it in their hearts; and will be their God, and they shall be my people.

And they shall teach no more every man his neighbor, and every man his brother, saying, Know the Lord: for they shall all know me, from the least of them unto the greatest of them, saith the Lord: for I will forgive their iniquity, and I will remember their sin no more.

This is the promise of the Holy Spirit in the minds of every man, where no one would have to tell another to know God or that they had done wrong, but everyone would know and understand in their hearts what was right and what was wrong.

Therefore, when the Holy Spirit takes over your life, as a married man or woman, He begins to teach you how to stay faithful to one another, and how to fight for your marriage. He teaches us how to flee from sexual immorality, and drug and alcohol abuse. He empowers us to be strong in the Spirit and dead to the flesh daily.

Joseph is an example of one who exhibited self-control and fleeing from the appearance of evil. He refused to lay with Potiphar's wife, because of his God and his boss (Genesis 37-50). In this present day, there are some who throw caution to the wind, giving in to lust and calling it love, engaging in sexual perversion, and at times excusing their behavior because of their supposed in-born inclinations. Meanwhile, the enemy is given access to take a seat in the corner of those hearts, and to plant seeds of destruction inside. When one has not given the Holy Spirit a chance to work in their lives, they leave room to be consumed by evil thoughts and will eventually fall for them. As sin continues, deception grows, so that sin no longer feels wrong. Do not give in to sin, and maintain your understanding of what is wrong and what is right. Abide by self-discipline, restraint, abstention and temperance, and keep them close to your heart. The Bible says to be angry but sin not. So even when provoked to anger, we must compose ourselves in a manner that seeks to please God first.

Self-control can be duly fulfilled by God's grace and our God said His grace is sufficient for us, even in weakness.

Steps Two and Three: Love and Obedience to God

In addition to self-control, subduing the flesh cannot be achieved if man does not obey God. To exhibit self-control in our lives means we have decided to be obedient to God.

What is Obedience?

According to the Google dictionary, to obey means to "comply with the command, direction, or request of a person or a law; submit to a person's authority or an institution". It could also mean "carrying out a set of commands, instructions, or statutes or behave in accordance with a general principle, natural law, spiritual law, etc.".

As children of God, we know there are consequences for disobedience, and in order to always be on the right side with God, we must be obedient to His commands. Remember that our God is a good God and whatever He says is for His children's best interest. God is Father and King over all, and every word He speaks becomes law. and as his subjects As His people, we are to be obedient to the Master's laid out statutes and plans.

Consider what the Psalmist said in Psalm 23:3b: "He leads me in the paths of righteousness, **for His name's sake.** (NKJV)"

The Lord leads us for His name's sake, not because He wants to subdue you or make you feel any less than He has created and called you to be. God's reputation is at stake if you do not succeed, and the only way to succeed in this Kingdom is by obeying the ordinances of the Holy God. Always bear in mind that the Lord has your best interest at heart. We still have an enemy who desires to destroy us, but because the devil knows that he cannot actually destroy us as God's children, he causes us to sin, separating us from the love of the Father. This is why, again, the Psalmist said in Psalm 5:8- "Lead me, O Lord, in thy righteousness because of mine enemies; make thy way straight before my face. (KJV)"

Righteous living is not just about you doing God's will, it is one of the ways to subdue every form of carnality in us, and defeat the kingdom of darkness. You are obedient to God so that you do not give the enemy access to your life and destiny. You choose to stay away from every form of pride, hard drugs, and sexual immorality because the Bible says that your body is the Lord's sanctuary. So, when your body is pure, the Spirit of the Lord can dwell within you, and the enemy cannot have a foothold because your heart is already occupied.

Therefore, children of God, understand that it is indeed within your capacity to overcome the desires of the flesh, by the grace of God Himself, through the power of the Holy Ghost in you.

As stated in previous chapters that the Lord does not necessarily delight in burnt offerings. After all, He said that when the children of Israel were delivered from the land of Egypt He did not request for sacrifice, all He requested for was their obedience. He wanted the children of Israel to do what He had commanded them to do without double checking what he said.

In I Samuel 15, the prophet, Samuel, told King Saul that obedience is better than sacrifice. God asked that the Amalekites be killed, every single one of them, down to the animals. He told the prophet that it was because the Amalekites were wicked to the children of Israel when they were coming out of Egypt. But Saul disobeyed and brought back king Agag (king of the Amalekites), including the best of their goats, sheep and oxen, stating that he was going to offer them as sacrifices to God. The Lord informed the prophet of King Saul's disobedience and was so unhappy that He said He regretted ever making Saul king over His people.

> *And Samuel said, Hath the Lord as great delight in burnt offerings and sacrifices, as in obeying the voice of the Lord? Behold, to obey is better than sacrifice, and to hearken than the fat of rams.*
>
> 1 Sam. 15:22

It is better to obey the voice of the Lord than to rebel like Lucifer, whose disobedience and rebellion caused him to be thrown down from heaven.

Deuteronomy 28:15–64 tells of all the curses that come upon us when we are disobedient to God. So, if ever someone told you that there are no consequences for sin without repentance, they lied.

Addressing obedience can make us think that God does not love us, but wants to enslave us with harsh rules and regulations that we may not have the ability to completely adhere to, but this is not so. God's Word is clear, that we love God because He first loved us (1 John 4:19). Think of it this way: wherever we find ourselves, whether as citizens of a country or institution, there are always laws and guidelines which must be obeyed. We obey them because we love our country and its citizens.

> *Then one of them, which was a lawyer, asked him a question, tempting him, and saying, Master, which is the great commandment in the law? Jesus said unto him, thou shalt love the Lord thy God with all thy heart, and with all thy soul, and with all thy mind. This is the first and great commandment. And the second is like unto it, thou shalt love thy neighbor as thyself. On these two commandments hang all the law and the prophets.*

Matt. 22:35-40 (KJV)

At this point, we should have an understanding that these laws were not merely made to subject us to obedience, but to also show that it is important to love both God and our neighbors. Subduing the flesh teaches you to control and restrain yourself from doing something that you would ordinarily love to do against yourself, someone else, and God. Take road rage for example. An accident or altercation can be avoided if both parties resist any urge to get out of their vehicle, argue, fight back, or even honk. You can be angry but not sin. Imagine that other people are like family. You would not be inclined to hurt your brother or sister. As a woman, it should not be my desire to cause a man to fall into sin by tempting him in any way. When we love God, and understand the purposes of His law, we do not take obeying Him, and loving Him, and or our neighbors, lightly.

Subduing the flesh restrains us and others from sinning. Through the work of the Holy Spirit, we see our body as the Lord's sanctuary/temple, and knowing that the same is true for other members of the Body of Christ. Keeping this in mind will help you to control your urge for sin, because you do not want to be the reason others fall into sin, and because you want to remain pure before the Lord, because of the love and sacrifice of our Savior Jesus Christ.

> *And whosoever shall offend one of these little ones that believe in me, it is better for him that a millstone were hanged about his neck, and he were cast into the sea.*
>
> Mark 9:42 KJV

God does not take it lightly when someone causes others to stumble. This is one reason why the enemy and his agents so often attack pastors and other spiritual leaders and teachers of God's Word, that they may be caused to say something contrary to what the Bible says. Being in leadership over the less spiritually mature, might cause them to fall for heresies or false doctrines.

As a child of God, it is important to prayerfully study the Word and allow the Holy Spirit function in our lives.

God loves us so much that He sent His only Son before the foundations of the earth to die for you and for me, for the redemption of our sins. He loves us so that even when we sin, He encourages us to come back to Him and ask for His mercies.

> *If my people, which are called by my name, shall humble themselves, and pray, and seek my face, and turn from their wicked ways; then will I hear from heaven, and will forgive their sin, and will heal their land.*
>
> 2 Chron. 7:14 KJV

Our God keeps wooing and chasing us with love and kindness, but some still choose to remain hard-hearted and follow the ways of this world which will only lead to death, after all 'the wages of sin is death' according to Romans 6:23.

As a wife desiring love from her husband, and as a husband desiring respect from his wife so does God in Heaven desire love and respect from us, His Bride. Without love, submission becomes difficult. So, we must learn to love God first, understand that He truly loves us, and obedience will follow. Love is the principal thing. Without love it is impossible to be yielded to the things of God.

Step Four: Loyalty to God

What does it mean to be loyal?

Loyalty means "giving or showing firm and constant support or allegiance to a person or institution", according to the Google Dictionary.

Wikipedia describes loyalty as "a devotion and faithfulness to a nation, cause, philosophy, country, group, or person".

When John the Baptist baptized the Jews, he said to them "Repent, for the kingdom of heaven is at hand." (John 3:2 NKJV)

The New Living Translation states, "Repent of your sins and turn to God, for the Kingdom of Heaven is near."

> Now when He was asked by the Pharisees when the kingdom of God would come, He answered them and said, "The kingdom of God does not come with observation; nor will they say, 'See here!' or 'See there!' For indeed, **the kingdom of God is within you.**"

Luke 17:20-21 (NKJV)

John and Jesus Christ both spoke of a Kingdom, in this Kingdom there is a King, and as God's children created in His image, we are citizens of this Kingdom.

Every kingdom has enemies, and battles to be fought. However, this is a victorious battle because of the death, resurrection, and ascension of Jesus Christ.

In other words, to succeed in this Kingdom, we are first to recognize that we cannot do without the Father who happens to be the King, Jesus Christ, the Son and Word, and the Holy Spirit.

Throughout the Old Testament, the Lord talked about a "new covenant", and the promise of the Holy Spirit.

> And it shall come to pass afterward, that I will pour out my spirit upon all flesh; and your sons and your daughters shall prophesy, your old men shall dream dreams, your young men shall see visions:

And also, upon the servants and upon the handmaids in those days will I pour out my spirit.

Joel 2:28-29 KJV

With the Holy Spirit's help, God's children bear the ability to go beyond simply obeying God's commands to also being loyal to His throne. There's something powerful about being loyal. Embedded in loyalty is love, respect, reverence, obedience, relationship, devotion, and faith. This is the point to which the Father desires to see His children reach: where we pledge allegiance to His Kingdom, and to doing His will. As a citizen of the Kingdom, we grow in love, genuine reverence, and devotion to the King, not just because we feel so, but because He said so, trusting that His Word is **law**. Then we can boldly declare Philippians 1:21 (KJV): "For me to live is Christ and to die is gain", and Galatians 2:20 (KJV):" I am crucified with Christ: nevertheless, I live; yet not I, but Christ liveth in me: and the life which I now live in the flesh I live by the faith of the Son of God, who loved me, and gave himself for me."

Serving God with loyalty and obedience goes far beyond the scope of pleasing men, but to pleasing the Almighty King.

So, whether people are looking or not, we are in constant submission to the commands, statutes, and regulations of the Kingdom of God.

In this generation, when people sometimes say one thing before you and another behind you, the virtue of loyalty has become increasingly hard to find. Like love, if you cannot love your brother, whom you can see, how can you love an invisible God? If you cannot diligently love, serve and obey your parents, institutions, etc., how can you declare yourself as loyal to the Kingdom of God, which you cannot see? At any given opportunity, you become a backstabber and a betrayer just for a small or fleeting alternative pleasure or false satisfaction.

Ask yourself, "Do I genuinely acknowledge the sacrifice of Jesus Christ on the cross for me?" Submission and loyalty to the kingdoms of the world puts us in a war zone. This may not be an easy thing to hear, but it is reality. God's children must comprehend that we are in a real battle with the enemy. Satan is working overtime to prove to God that we are not capable of the responsibilities that He has set before us, but God, in His infinite mercy, looks beyond our flaws and asks us to draw nearer to Him, even in our sin. This is why in this Kingdom in which our Father is Spirit, we are commanded to worship Him in Spirit and in truth (John 4:23).

Our fall to sin allows Satan to mock God. We can use Job as a case study, when God called Satan's attention to him, asking, "Have you considered my servant Job?"

> *And the Lord said unto Satan, Hast thou considered my servant Job, that there is none like him in the earth, a perfect and an upright man, one that feareth God, and escheweth evil?*

> Job 1:8 (KJV)

Satan began to explain to God why he thought Job was faithful to God, stating that God put a hedge around Job, making him untouchable. but little did he know, however, that Job had such faith and love for God that he declared, "though he slay me, yet will I trust in him: but I will maintain mine own ways before him. (Job 13:15 KJV)

For those of us who might not know Job's full story, let me give you a little background. Job was a man highly favored by God. In fact, he was the richest within that entire area where he lived, with seven sons and three daughters, seven thousand sheep, three thousand camels, five hundred oxen, and five female donkeys. He was so rich with blessings and joy, He always offered burnt sacrifices to God for purification and sanctification, for himself and his children, for sins that they may have committed in their hearts that he was not aware of. Job loved God very much and understood the importance of staying away from sin and iniquity. God Himself spoke of Job as a righteous man, upright and blameless before him, but Satan said Job was only faithful to God because of all that God had given to him.

> There once was a man named Job who lived in the land of Uz. He was blameless—a man of complete integrity. He feared God and stayed away from evil. He had seven sons and three daughters. He owned 7,000 sheep, 3,000 camels, 500 teams of oxen, and 500 female donkeys. He also had many servants. He was, in fact, the richest person in that entire area. Job's sons would take turns preparing feasts in their homes, and they would also invite their three sisters to celebrate with them. When these celebrations ended—sometimes after several days—Job would purify his children. He would get up early in the morning and offer a burnt offering for each of them. For Job said to himself, "Perhaps my children have sinned and have cursed God in their hearts." This was Job's regular practice.

Job 1:1-5 (NLT)

God allowed Satan to test Job to see if he was truly loyal to his Kingdom or just because of the gifts of the Kingdom he had access to. But Job saw beyond the things God had blessed him

The Mastery of Subduing the Flesh

with, and he spoke of his test from the point of love and loyalty to God. What if Job had fallen for Satan's tricks? God knew Job's heart, and knew that He could trust him. This is a testament to how our love for God should also help us to put the flesh under submission, not because we have the full ability to do so, but because when we decide in our heart not to do the bidding of the flesh, the Holy Spirit then comes and assists us, giving us the grace and strength to overcome. If God is able to pledge His allegiance to us as His people, are we not supposed to do same for this Kingdom to which we belong? Yes, we are imperfect, but we are striving for perfection.

Study these words from God to the children of Israel. I suggest the practice of putting your own name any place that you find the word "Israel" or "Jacob", and even read it out loud to yourself:

> "But you, Israel, are My servant,
> Jacob whom I have chosen,
> The descendants of Abraham My friend.
> You whom I have taken from the ends of the earth,
> And called from its farthest regions,
> And said to you,
> 'You are My servant,
> I have chosen you and have not cast you away:
> Fear not, for I am with you;
> Be not dismayed, for I am your God.
> I will strengthen you,
> Yes, I will help you,
> I will uphold you with My righteous right hand.'
> Isa. 41:8-10 (KJV)
>
> *King David says a prayer to God, making promises to Him, but when you read properly you realize*

that he was declaring his allegiance to God's government.

O God, thou art my God; early will I seek thee: my soul thirsteth for thee, my flesh longeth for thee in a dry and thirsty land, where no water is;

To see thy power and thy glory, so as I have seen thee in the sanctuary.

Because thy lovingkindness is better than life, my lips shall praise thee.

Thus, will I bless thee while I live: I will lift up my hands in thy name.

My soul shall be satisfied as with marrow and fatness; and my mouth shall praise thee with joyful lips:

When I remember thee upon my bed, and meditate on thee in the night watches.

Because thou hast been my help, therefore in the shadow of thy wings will I rejoice.

My soul followeth hard after thee: thy right hand upholdeth me

Ps. 63:1-5 (KJV)

For those who are married, they say their vows before the altar of God, to forsake all others. As born–again, Spirit-filled Christians, we strive to keep that same vow. Why do we struggle to keep our vows? Mostly because we do not want to hurt our spouses, we want to keep their trust, and also out of compassion and love, because we would not want them to cheat on us, so we strive to stay faithful and committed. This is what it is like with God and subduing the flesh. Do not merely consider yourself and how you feel, but also consider the love of the Master, and the schemes of the enemy. If Jesus loves us too much to ever fail us, we should offer the same love for Him in return.

The Mastery of Subduing the Flesh

Something that I often say is that Christianity is one religion (Although it is not so much a religion as a lifestyle. For the sake of understanding, though, let's call it 'religion'.) where the One we serve pledges allegiance to His subjects. We, the King's subjects, must pledge allegiance to the Kingdom and stand by it. God says, "I will never leave you nor forsake you, be not dismayed, be of good courage. (Heb. 13:5)" He gave everything for you and me, and is surely saddened when we do not feel the same way. I consider my relationship with God a love affair; He is faithful to me, so I will be loyal and faithful to Him also. He is the head of my life, so I must love and serve Him in order to put the kingdom of darkness to shame. We must understand that the power of God is far greater than anything in this world, and the righteous are the true partakers of God's greatness. We are all God's children, yes. But God's mighty blessings are for those who fight the good fight and carry their cross daily. We must understand that fighting the good fight is not only preaching and evangelizing. Jesus Christ told His disciples that whoever wants to follow Him must take up their cross daily. Subduing the flesh's activities is taking up your cross daily. It is fighting hard and telling the devil that nothing is going to separate us from the love of the Father. We must hold on, looking unto Jesus Christ, the author and the Finisher of our faith. Do not let the devil win in your life; what do you desire that the Lord of hosts cannot give to you? He made you in His image, sacrificed His own Son before the foundation of the world, and calls us His own special people–a chosen generation. The only way to repay God is to be in His corner, to love, and obey His commands. Because we are so loved we also should love sincerely with everything within us. The Bible said that the law can be summed up into two simple commandments. The first is to love the Lord your God with all of your heart, soul, and might, and the second is to love your neighbors as you love yourself (Matthew 22:37-40). As simple as this may sound it has obviously been proven that it is very difficult on our own. We hear of sons killing their parents, neighbors gunning down neighbors, friends envious of friends and doing all they can to ruin one another. But thank God for the Holy Spirit, the Comforter that the Father has sent to us to teach and guide us into all truths, with no exceptions. Ask the Lord anything and He will reveal it to you. He loves you that much. Inquire of Him, according to Jeremiah 33: 3, and He will reveal every hidden thing. Pay no attention to that age-long enemy that has already been defeated, who knows his end and wants you to join him there. Do not be deceived, the place burning with fire and brimstone was not created for God's children, but for those angels that rebelled against Him. How then can we allow this devil to lie to us about what is clearly stated in the Word? When you sin, come and ask for mercy and I will forgive you, says the Lord of Hosts. Praise the Lord, in Christ, there is room for restoration even though the heart of our Father breaks when we sin. He is ever ready to accept us back into His kingdom when we have genuinely repented.

Children of God, understand your weaknesses and seek the Holy Spirit to come and give you the required strength to conquer those weaknesses. The Lord advises us to flee from all appearances of evil, because although our spirit is willing, the flesh is weak.

> *Blessed is the man*
> *Who walks not in the counsel of the ungodly,*
> *Nor stands in the path of sinners,*
> *Nor sits in the seat of the scornful;*
> *But his delight is in the law of the Lord,*
> *And in His law, he meditates day and night.*
> Ps. 1:1-2 (NKJV)

The Bible says "Do not be deceived, bad company corrupts good manners", therefore do not put yourself in a position where you are in a battle to sin, but overcome sin by staying away, and running far from signs of temptation.

> *Be not deceived: evil communications corrupt good manners.*
>
> 1 Cor. 15:33 (KJV)
>
> *Abstain from all appearance of evil.*
>
> 1 Thess. 5:22 (KJV)

You are not as tough on your own as you may believe yourself to be; the Bible says even the very elect will fall, so watch and pray so you do not fall into temptation. By the power in the blood of Jesus, you have been redeemed. Our Amazing God has told us that He will be our strength in weakness. This implies that if you act tough, and think you can save yourself by yourself, then disaster looms. You know God does not want us to do anything without Him, because he said that we can do nothing without Him.

> *For there shall arise false Christs, and false prophets, and shall shew great signs and wonders; insomuch that, if it were possible, they shall deceive the very elect.*
>
> Matt. 24:24 (KJV)

> *I am the vine, ye are the branches: He that abideth in me, and I in him, the same bringeth forth much fruit: **for without me ye can do nothing.***

John 15:5 (KJV)

Only loyalty to God can keep you from falling to sin. Our love for God will help us to subdue the activities of the flesh, because this is how we show God that we love Him.

Our minds have to be put under subjection to the things of the Spirit.

> *I beseech you therefore, brethren, by the mercies of God, that ye present your bodies a living sacrifice, holy, acceptable unto God, which is your reasonable service.*
> *And be not conformed to this world: but be ye transformed by the renewing of your mind, that ye may prove what is that good, and acceptable, and perfect, will of God.*

Rom. 12:1-2 (KJV)

> *For the eyes of the Lord runs to and fro throughout the whole earth, to show Himself strong on **behalf of those who are loyal to Him.***

2 Chron. 16:9 (NKJV)

Renew your mind by changing your thoughts. Your mind is a powerful tool in the hands of the Creator, so allow Him to make the change for you, as you make a decision in your heart to walk according to the leading of the Holy Spirit.

Section Four

Message to the Unbelieving

God created man in his image, but man's sin caused mankind to fall, and the authority that God gave us was passed on to the age-long enemy who was spoken of in Revelation 12:9.

You may not believe this, but you are included in this story. After the fall, it became hard for man to truly please God, hence the arrival of Jesus Christ to earth to redeem you and me from our sins, causing God to look at us through the blood of His Son that was sacrificed on the cross. You are a part of those that the Lord redeemed. Our strengths and weaknesses make up who we are, as a human being, we have to believe that no one is perfect. Sometimes we are guilty of falling into temptation due to our shortcomings. Our weaknesses could come in different forms: gluttony, sexual sins, or addiction. The serpent who was present in the garden has the advantage of time. Satan is considered powerful by some because they have not tried or tested the power of Jesus Christ. In our imperfections, the death of Jesus makes us perfect. The fall of man made us sinful in nature, but the death of Jesus Christ came to restore the newness in man.

> **"No one is righteous—**
> **not even one.**
> No one is truly wise;
> no one is seeking God.
> All have turned away;
> all have become useless.
> No one does good,
> not a single one."
> "Their talk is foul, like the stench from an open grave.
> Their tongues are filled with lies."
> "Snake venom drips from their lips."
> "Their mouths are full of cursing and bitterness."
> "They rush to commit murder.
> Destruction and misery always follow them.
> They don't know where to find peace."
> "They have no fear of God at all."

Rom. 3:11-18 (NKJV)

In Christianity, it is acknowledged that no one is perfect or righteous before God. It is only the blood of Jesus Christ which serves as an atonement for all our wrongdoing. In our humanity, this concept can be difficult to grasp, but the Bible says we have to receive by faith. I urge you to see past what the world has told you. For in human nature, there is really nothing but sin and evil. So, if someone tells you to search for the best version of yourself inside of you, that fellow lied to you. Look around and you will see that we are here today because we have been told that it's alright to give in to your weaknesses, or to do whatever makes you happy. This very statement is what is landing God's children in hell. Do you not know that Satan plays with your mind, he takes advantage of what you watch and listen to and keeps your mind on those things? Do not take your thoughts and imagination for granted. It is from there that your cravings and desires first begin, before they manifest for all to see.

> *Keep your heart with all diligence,*
> *For out of it spring the issues of life.*

Prov. 4:23 (KJV)

> *Finally, brethren, whatsoever things are true, whatsoever things are honest, whatsoever things are just, whatsoever things are pure, whatsoever things are lovely, whatsoever things are of good report; if there be any virtue, and if there be any praise, think on these things.*

Phil. 4:8 (KJV)

Something I have noticed, is some people behave as though they do not need the love of Christ because they have money, power, and fame. You are loved, and life after death is real. Think about where you would spend eternity. Satan knows his end and he is doing all he can to take as many of God's favorites with him. You are God's favorite. His breath is in you, and if he takes his breath out of you that's death, which is something that Satan would not be able to help you with. You are not excluded from those the Lord created in His image, no matter how deep in sin you may be or how far gone you may have traveled in darkness. The blood of Jesus Christ rescues and redeems all. Find a way to believe these words.

> *For what shall it profit a man, if he shall gain the whole world, and lose his own soul?*
> *Or what shall a man give in exchange for his soul?*

The Mastery of Subduing the Flesh

    Mark 8:36-37 (KJV)

There is so much more to life than bread and butter. There is love, contentment, sacrifice, commitment, and more. We need to turn from our sinful ways and not allow Satan to continue to feed our ego and weaknesses. Take a stand with Jesus Christ today, and declare that He is your Lord and Savior, so the powers of darkness know you stand. Begin to study the Word so you can walk in the light of Jesus.

By the empowering and equipping of the Holy Spirit, serving God becomes easy, from a point of love and loyalty. You stand strong so that the enemy may be put to shame. When you surrender yourself to Jesus Christ by accepting this new life, which He has freely given through the cross, you become a new creation, and a citizen of the Kingdom of God which is within you. Do not put off the Spirit of conviction within you, for this is the Spirit of God at work inside of you. You are now a part of the new covenant when you confess Him with your mouth as your Lord and Savior.

The spirit of unbelief has kept God's children in darkness, Jesus said, "And when He has come, He will convict the world of sin, and of righteousness, and of judgment: of sin, because they do not believe in Me". This statement simply means that we remain in sin because we do not know Him.

Today, I introduce Jesus Christ to you. He is our Redeemer, the God who does not keep record of wrongs, our Restorer, and Deliverer. Jesus Christ delivers us from death as we cry for mercy today, turn to Him, the sacrifice of animals or any other form of ritual is no longer required. Jesus conquered death, took over the keys of death, and the enemy is no longer in control. Satan is just following a script written by God, so nothing He does is new or surprising to God. God is Almighty, and had this figured out before the foundation of the earth. If Satan knew, he would not have tempted men into crucifying Jesus Christ. He is a fool and a defeated foe. None of us can afford to leave our lives in the hands of someone who has already been defeated, is being defeated, and will be defeated again.

> *We are made right with God by placing our faith in Jesus Christ. And this is true for everyone who believes, no matter who we are.*

Rom. 3:22 (NLT)

> *Now the just shall live by faith: but if any man draw back, my soul shall have no pleasure in him.*

Heb. 10:38 (KJV)

It is clearly stated that the just shall live by faith. The words of the Bible are true, and should not be ignored. Jesus Christ commanded us to trust in Him, as He is truth personified; in Him, there is no lie. The enemy comes to steal, kill and destroy. He destroys you at the peak of your life, unless you partner with him in the destruction of others, then he may cause you to live longer. One day, though, it will be your moment of destruction too. Partner with Jesus Christ today, and become a better version of yourself and help win others to this Kingdom, save your soul from hell, and enjoy the life Jesus sacrificed Himself for.

Jude 24-25

Now unto him that is able to keep you from falling, and to present you faultless before the presence of his glory with exceeding joy,

To the only wise God our Saviour, be glory and majesty, dominion and power, both now and ever. Amen.